Becoming the New You

#1 International Best Selling Author
DR. DONATO PERRICCI

Published By: DNP Publishing

Library of Congress Cataloging-in-Publication Data has been applied for

Scripture taken from the New King James Version®. Copyright © 1982 by Thomas Nelson. Used by permission. All rights reserved. Scripture quotations marked (NIV) are taken from the Holy Bible, New International Version®, NIV®. Copyright © 1973, 1978, 1984, 2011 by Biblica, Inc.® Used by permission of Zondervan. All rights reserved worldwide. www.zondervan.com The "NIV" and "New International Version" are trademarks registered in the United States Patent and Trademark Office by Biblica, Inc.®

ISBN: 979-8-8691-0889-0

PRINTED IN THE UNITED STATES OF AMERICA

Becoming the New You is geared towards anyone wanting to become better in their life, whether they are Christians or not. This book leads you down the path of salvation and keeps it simple to understand for those who are seeking it. Most of the scripture references being used are from the New King James unless otherwise stated. This book also gives you practical tools and directions to follow that will help you to succeed in life and help you build a better foundation to grow.

TABLE OF CONTENTS

FOREWORD

By Dr. Pamela Henkel

We all get to choose whether we will live by Design or by default; for so many, this concept of choice has remained unattainable. We all have a God-given Destiny to fulfill while we are here on this earth, yet daily, people everywhere live in bondage and below the poverty line of their divine purpose. Challenging situations and life circumstances are more real now than ever, which is why people need to hope that change is possible. Living life by Design is not impossible. It is easier than you may think. The hardest part is choosing to let God take the wheel of your life. "Becoming The New You" addresses this topic boldly. Dr. Donato Perricci loves transforming lives by introducing people to the God of Transformation.

I have known Dr. Donato Perricci (or Dr/Pastor D as I like to call him) for 12+ years. We have worked in ministry together as well as business. I was his pastor for many years, and now he is mine. Donato is a close friend; he is the real deal. I am honored to write this Forward and endorse this incredible book!

"Victorious Living," Donato shares, "is all about your mindset." Dr. Donato believes that, first and foremost, this begins by finding who you are in Christ. Dr. Donato lives his life empowering others to discover just that and embrace a God-given, victorious mindset. Having grappled with many life obstacles, Dr. Donato preaches, writes, and teaches with passion and understanding.

Born in Wisconsin, Donato experienced significant loss by the age of five and then came into a broken family at the age of nine. He then found himself growing up in Gary, Indiana, during the later part of middle school and the start of his high school years. Donato then moved around, ending up in Minnesota. Where Donato suffered many hardships that children and teens should not experience. Dr. Donato teaches out his wealth of life experience and knowledge. He has become a Senior Pastor, International best-selling author and motivational speaker, successful businessman and business coach with over 30 years in Corporate America.

In the following pages of this book, Donato will train you in the art of self-mastery. He will enlighten you with timeless, eternal truths. You will receive precepts and steps to embrace all God has for you. When the pupil is ready, the teacher appears. "Becoming The New You" is the tool you need. I encourage you to say YES to God, your dreams, and yourself. Read this book, do what Pastor D says to do. A great change will happen, and then you, my friend, will help change the world.

To Your Greatness,

Dr. Pamela Henkel

Leader, Energizer, Philanthropist

https://linktr.ee/Purposewithpamela

INTRODUCTION

It doesn't matter what time of the year it is to start fresh and make new commitments to improve yourself. Everyone has made a New Year's resolution at some point. Unfortunately, many people don't keep commitments or resolutions for one reason or another. It often has something to do with the habits that they already have. It can be hard to create a new habit or possibly get rid of the one that they are trying to overcome. This book will give you many different insights into who we are as people and so much more. I pray that you will find something in this book that will help you break the cycle that you have been in if you need it and give you some hope, encouragement, and a new perspective that will get you on the right track.

This book covers many things that will help your journey to Becoming the New You! We first need to set a good foundation to get your mindset right and then give you the tools you need. There are many steps or questions you will be asked along the way. Becoming the New You is a type of workbook or journal; please make sure to track your progress along the way. Doing this will help you to look back into the future and see how far you have come.

CHAPTER 1

Getting to know yourself through God

This chapter is about getting to know yourself through God. God, plain and simple, is LOVE! God loves you and wants to have a relationship with you, as stated in John 3:16-17. It is that Unconditional Love that forgives us, as well as His Grace and Mercy that He has towards us. However, it is your choice to have a relationship with Him. I believe wholeheartedly this relationship is vital to finding and Becoming the New You!

I wanted to start this book by us hearing from God in the Scriptures to lay a foundation on which we can build.

As it says in Isaiah 28:16

16 Therefore thus says the Lord GOD:

"Behold, I lay in Zion a stone for a foundation,

A tried stone, a precious cornerstone, a sure foundation;

Whoever believes will not act hastily.

The key here is that we need to believe and not act hastily, as it says. So, please take your time with this book and make sure that you take things to heart as you read. You can be that precious cornerstone that God uses to build upon. I believe that God is always trying to encourage us to grow in Him and become a better person all the time, not just at the start of the new year. Now is as good as any time to start. You just need the right frame of mind Keep in mind that this is a process and will take time and effort. You cannot just flip a switch, and everything is just perfect. You will have to put some work into it, but we can do everything through Christ. Just don't give up!

A good example of this can be found in:

2 Corinthians 3:16-18… *[16] Nevertheless when one turns to the Lord, the veil is taken away. [17] Now the Lord is the Spirit; and where the Spirit of the Lord is, there is liberty. [18] But we all, with unveiled face, beholding as in a mirror*

the glory of the Lord, are being transformed into the same image from glory to glory, just as by the Spirit of the Lord.

We are constantly being transformed by something for good or bad. We, however, get to choose which, so why not let it be from Glory to Glory by the Spirit of the Lord as stated here? Did you catch the part at the beginning where it talks about one turning to the Lord? This is essential to transforming your life and getting it on the right track. Knowing Jesus as Lord and Savior is the first part of getting your life on track and making it better. Having the Holy Spirit to guide you helps to give that extra help that we all need from time to time in our lives. If you do not know Jesus as Lord and Savior, I encourage you to go towards the back of the book where I have put a simple Salvation Prayer that you can say and confess Jesus as Lord and Savior. Trust me, knowing Jesus will change your life and will be able to be the strength you need to walk through life.

When we receive Jesus as Lord, several things happen. One is that the burden we have been carrying around is lifted when we are forgiven for our sins. We become more aware of our sins and that God's Unconditional Love has forgiven us and is now leading us in His Spirit of Truth! Then, when we are filled with the Holy Spirit, we have the Spirit to help us and guide us to walk uprightly. We then also get the Liberty that the passage talks about. Therefore, we must also invite the Holy Spirit into our hearts to lead us in this Spirit of Truth.

We are told this by Jesus in John 16 verses 12-15: [12] *"I still have many things to say to you, but you cannot bear them now.* [13] *However, when He, the Spirit of truth, has come, He will guide you into all truth; for He will not speak on His own authority, but whatever He hears He will speak; and He will tell you things to come.* [14] *He will glorify Me, for He will take of what is Mine and declare it to you.* [15] *All things that the Father has are Mine. Therefore I said that He will take of Mine and declare it to you.*

As we need to have Jesus in our lives, we also need to receive the Holy Spirit. If you looked at the Salvation Prayer in the back of the book, you would have seen I also include asking the Holy Spirit into our hearts. Why not have all that God has to offer us? The Holy Spirit is there to show us the way and be that Spirit of Truth to guide us in our lives. So many people struggle to find themselves and overcome many of life's challenges. Let's be honest: life is not always easy. There are many things we face every day. With the Holy Spirit, our choices and decisions can be made easier by knowing that we have peace which comes from the Holy Spirit guiding us in that Spirit of Truth.

Sometimes, even if we are already Christians who are saved, set free, and filled with the Holy Spirit, we may lose sight of the things of God as we get busy with our day-to-day lives. This book might be the nudge you need today to get back on track with your relationship with God. God hasn't forgotten about you, but you can tie His hands by trying to do things on your own. God will not override your free will. The saying let go and let God is true. Sometimes, we need to give up and surrender, hand over whatever it is to God and then forget about it. I can't begin to tell you how many times I have had to do this myself. If you are at all like me with a Type A Personality, you can understand that this is not easy, but I promise you that if you can surrender whatever it is to God and lay it down at the feet of Jesus and leave it there; God will help you. The trick is not to pick it back up and nurture it all over again as all your effort then would be for not.

As this book is going to be interactive, there are going to be many questions and tasks along the way that you can document your progress, so be honest and then later down the road you can look back and see the progress that you have made.

<u>Question Time:</u>

Let me ask you a few questions about what we have covered so far.

Have you accepted Jesus into your heart?   If so, when?

Have you accepted the Holy Spirit? If so, when?

Or are you a Christian already and need a reboot?

Do you forget about God and get caught up in life? What changes can you make?

Is there something that you need to let go and hand over to God?

Now, getting back to the passage of 2 Corinthians. The veil that is being talked about is interesting. It was in reference to Moses when he met with God. Moses spent time with God face to face and when he came down from the mountain, he shone brightly from being in God's presence. The veil that is being talked about was used to cover Moses' face, basically so that the people would not be afraid, as Moses was still shining from being in the presence of God. They did not understand spiritual things. The veil would be removed as the radiance of God's presence passed away from him.

When you are saved and filled with the Holy Spirit, your eyes open to the Spirit of Truth and the spiritual realm, which is another veil of sorts. You can be in the presence of God and be filled with His Glory, just as Moses was but not need the veil anymore. Today, because of Jesus, the veil is removed, as there is no need for separation from God anymore. This is also a reference to the Veil that was in the Temple that separated the Holy of Holies. When Jesus died, that veil in the temple was torn as the redemption for our sins was completed once and for all when He became for us the Sacrificial Lamb to take away the sins of the world. This means that we can come to God anytime. When we choose to spend time with Him, we get to know His heart more and more. As we understand the heart of God, we then start to be transformed into the person that He sees we can be. God believes in you, so it is time that you begin to believe in yourself!

It is your time to shine! God wants great things for you, but it starts with getting to know Him first.

- Start to have a daily prayer conversation with God and to get to know Him.
- Read the Bible, as this is also a great way to get to know Him. After all it was written through Him.
- Praise and Worship, which helps you to get aligned quickly with His presence.

Let His presence fill you and you will go from glory to glory. This will not only transform your life with God, but you will start to see things in your day-to-day lives begin to line up, and your goal goals, dreams, and visions will come to pass.

<u>Question Time:</u>

These questions are similar but are different, as one is here and now and the other is more of a plan over time.

What can you do every day to draw closer to God?

What are you going to do so you can move from glory to glory? Meaning from where you are to where you want to go.

CHAPTER 2
Getting Past Ourselves

In this chapter, we will learn to get past ourselves as we delve into understanding how God sees us. When we start to see ourselves as God sees us, we then put behind us the things that no longer serve us from our past.

We start by looking at Romans 8:1 - *There is therefore now no condemnation to those who are in Christ Jesus, who do not walk according to the flesh, but according to the Spirit.*

Now that you have accepted Jesus and the Holy Spirit into your life, it is essential not to look back at former things. As people we tend to look back at all the wrong things we have done or all the junk that we have been through. We must stop doing this! It will keep us stuck in our past. Jesus has the answers we need. God love us and Jesus died for our sins, and we <u>have been</u> forgiven them.

Have been, which is underlined here, means that it has already been done and is in the past! If God can forgive us, then we need to forgive ourselves also. We may not be able to forget our past as easy as God does; but we need to put it behind us and move forward if we are to become the person that God knows and sees when He looks at us.

This is explained well in 2 Corinthians 5:17-19... *[17] Therefore, if anyone is in Christ, he is a new creation; old things have passed away; behold, all things have become new. [18] Now all things are of God, who has reconciled us to Himself through Jesus Christ, and has given us the ministry of reconciliation, [19] that is, that God was in Christ reconciling the world to Himself, not imputing their trespasses to them, and has committed to us the word of reconciliation.*

We were forgiven when we accepted Jesus into our hearts and God no longer sees our sinful ways. That is how we have become that "new creation" we read about. Jesus now has set us free and reconciled us to Him. We no longer need to be bound up by our sins and let them run or even ruin our lives. Now you can put away your past and have a new clean slate to work with as God has wiped away your sins. It says in this passage, "Old things have passed away; behold, behold, all things have become new." This doesn't mean it will be easy, but you can start off clean and fresh at any point when you ask for that forgiveness. You can then start to look at things the way that God looks at them and get a new perspective on life.

Question Time:

What is the baggage from your past that you should let go of or something you need to step away from?

Is there something that you need to forgive yourself for?

What are you going to do with your Clean New Slate?

The space between our ears (which is our minds) can be our own worst enemy. We may think back to the past on something or even dwell there. Not to mention that the devil will try to whisper in your ears at times, trying to remind you of your past. All you need to do is rebuke him and remind him of his future and that he is defeated. The devil is a liar, so do not listen or be led away by his tricks. We have spent too much of our lives listening to him. We are a new creation now in Christ, and we do not need to be held down by our past or our old sins that once again we are forgiven of.

We see in 1 Corinthians 2:16 that we have the mind of Christ: *For "who has known the mind of the LORD that he may instruct Him?" But we have the mind of Christ.*

In this verse, we can see that we have the mind of Christ. We now belong to Him and are joint heirs with Him. Everything that Christ has is also ours. Likewise, what we have belongs to Him, so use it wisely! All we need to do then is receive and know we belong to Him and He to us.

Here is another way to look at it in Romans 15:5-6: *5 Now may the God of patience and comfort grant you to be like-minded toward one another, according to Christ Jesus, 6 that you may with one mind and one mouth glorify the God and Father of our Lord Jesus Christ.*

Jesus taught us many things, but He often pointed back to His Father and would say that He only does what He see His Father do. If we now belong to Him and have His mind, we become like-minded as the scripture says. Simply put, we need to keep God first in all things.

Sometimes though, our minds still wonder so let's look at Philippians 4:6-7: [6] *Be anxious for nothing, but in everything by prayer and supplication, with thanksgiving, let your requests be made known to God;* [7] *and the peace of God, which surpasses all understanding, will guard your hearts and minds through Christ Jesus.*

There is a lot to this passage but believe it or not, our hearts and minds are linked. This gives us a guide to go by when things start to get overwhelming, and we start to get anxious, which is really another word for fear. Prayer is an integral part of our relationship with God, but also as we see here, it allows us to come to Him and get some stuff off our chest. When we do this, we need to then do what it says and be thankful that God has heard our prayers and know that He will answer them. Too often, people go back to God with the same things over and over (confession, I have done it also). We need to know and believe that God is not hard of hearing but has heard our request. God doesn't need a hearing aid! Once we have faith and believe that He has heard us, we know He will answer our prayers. Then that peace of God comes upon us and will relieve that burden.

I mentioned that our minds and hearts are linked. It is all about what we let into our minds and how long it takes to get into our hearts.

Matthew 6:21, *For where your treasure is, there your heart will be also.*

Jesus also said something like it later in Matthew 12:34, *Brood of vipers! How can you, being evil, speak good things? For out of the abundance of the heart the mouth speaks.*

Jesus clarifies that whatever comes out of our mouth comes from the heart. But how did it get there in the first place? If it is bad, then it is just our stinking thinking, some of which came from our sinful ways and the devil lying to us. Some of it may have been taught to us and we need to unlearn it. Therefore, we need the mind of Christ.

As a thought comes into our minds, we must figure out whether it is good or bad. If it is good, then OK, keep it there, and if it starts to bear fruit, we can allow it to become part of who we are, and then it gets into our hearts. If bad, however, we cannot allow that thing any room in our minds and need to cast it out, so it does not take root. This is how sin gets in and snowballs into something more prominent over time.

Question Time:

Is there something that you are anxious about?

Is there something that you need to get your mind right about?

What is in your heart and how does it come out?

What are you going to do next with what you just learned?

This all boils down to having an attitude of gratitude. It is no different with our daily lives and when we pray to God about something. Weren't you grateful for being saved and set free from the sin that once bound you up? Or, put another way, are you thankful for all of what you have currently?

An uncommon situation requires an uncommon response. You're not praising God for the storm that you are in. You are praising Him in spite of it! The depth of your praise determines the magnitude of your breakthrough, and our God is the God of the Breakthrough!!!

If the breakthrough was here and happened – How would you react? Would you not rejoice and be thankful? So why don't we act that way all the time? If we can change our attitude to that of an attitude of gratitude how much sooner are we going to receive our breakthrough and blessing? Begin to laugh, rejoice or praise God for what He has done and be thankful.

It is all about having the right mindset. There is nothing wrong with wanting more and having goals, dreams, and visions of the future, we need to be thankful for what we have, and the rest will fall into place. Once we can get past ourselves and have a better attitude about things, God can move more freely in our lives. God wants us to have the desires of our hearts and to be richly blessed.

What are the things you want? Is it ok to want them? The things that are right and just and pure, like our goals and dreams for our lives are ok to want. It says in the Word that God grants us the desires of our hearts! Do you know why? It is because He has placed them there. God is the one that gives us the dreams to want more and to reach higher. There is nothing wrong with wanting to succeed in life. In fact, this is how God can work on your behalf and bless you.

Question Time: (there is space to write in the back of the book also)

What are some of the things that you are thankful for?

Do you thank God for them?

Is there anything more that you can do to show an Attitude of Gratitude towards God and others?

How is everything that you have learned in this chapter going to change your prayer time with God and better your relationship with Him?

CHAPTER 3

Body, Soul, and Spirit

Ok, we have begun laying a good foundation. We need to continue to build on this. As we learn more about who we are in Christ. We need to understand more about who we really are. Each one of us is a spiritual being with a soul (which is also our mind, will and emotions) and we live in a body. This may sound odd to some, but just as there is God the Father, Jesus Christ His Son, and the Holy Spirit which makes three in one, we are the same way. We are made in the image of God. God breathed life into us which is our spirit. We can have the mind of Christ as we have read about. Then our bodies are the temple that it all resides in. Learning more about who we are is our next step. We will then be able to better ourselves and work on Becoming the New You. Understanding who we are will bring balance to our lives.

Starting with 1 Thessalonians 5:23-24 to back up everything, *23 Now may the God of peace Himself sanctify you completely; and may your whole spirit, soul, and body be preserved blameless at the coming of our Lord Jesus Christ. 24 He who calls you is faithful, who also will do it.*

This shows us that we are that three parts being and God wants us to be a whole and complete person. We then need to understand all these parts and take care of them properly. It also says that God has called you and that He is faithful. We need to do our part so God can do His part. If God has called us, He will equip us. As we explore each part separately, we will then learn more, and it will help us to do God's work.

Body:

People commonly look at themselves as their physical body. It is our outward appearance that we see, so that is who we think we are. So, let's start here as it will be the easiest part for us to relate. We all know the saying you are what you eat. This is true and applies to all aspects of our identity and the three parts of who we are. We can then understand that the food we put into our bodies will affect us. Just as going to the doctor or working out to keep our bodies in shape makes a difference in keeping us physically healthy.

Let's read at least one passage about what God's word says about the body.

1 Corinthians 6:19-20, [19] *Or do you not know that your body is the temple of the Holy Spirit who is in you, whom you have from God, and you are not your own?* [20] *For you were bought at a price; therefore glorify God in your body and in your spirit, which are God's.*

This passage gets deep if you let it. What we need to glean from it is now that we are saved and filled with the Holy Spirit, we need to take better care of ourselves. You could say that anything that would cause yourself harm, don't do it. Likewise, things that would be good for your body we should do. We tend to overlook even simple things that are good for the body. For example, though it may be silly, as I am writing this my hands really need some lotion on them. I say this to get us thinking as we tend to let certain things slide from time to time, thinking we will get to them. We need to make a conscious effort to do certain things and stop putting them off. So this, then, is a good segway into the next part of who we are in the Soul.

Soul:

Our Souls must be the most complex part of who we are. We have learned that we can have the mind of Christ. We also need to ensure we are feeding it the right things. However, we need to understand that our soul makes up our mind, both conscious and unconscious as well as our will and emotions. The thinking part of what we consider our mind is made up of both conscious and unconscious.

To cover it a little, it is like when I talked about things going from our minds to our hearts in the last chapter. So, our unconscious mind is always picking up things that we do not realize or think about. This can also be where our habits are, as most of the time with habits, we don't put forth much of a conscious effort when doing them and tend to link up with our bodies as muscle memory.

As you can see then this is something that is inside of us like what is in our hearts. The problem is that we have other things in our unconscious minds that we have allowed to be programmed there. If we hear things repeatedly and then start to believe them, it gets programmed into us, be it good or bad. This may have started when we were kids, be it coming from our parents or peers. Unfortunately, we seem to believe those bad reports we hear more often than not. We need to start believing the good report from God that says we are more than a conqueror in Christ Jesus and that we can do all things through Him who loves us. God loves us and wants the best for us.

We then need to reprogram ourselves. But how can we do that? By taking things into your conscious mind over and over. You may even want to speak out affirmations to help with this. Then, you can start to unroot the old negative idea and replace it with a positive one. This conscious effort of repetition will begin to seep its way into your unconscious and, over time, root out the bad that was once there. You must also stop the bad confessions in your life like "I am so stupid" or "I always get sick this time of year." This list could go on and on, but hopefully, you get the idea here. Stop the negative talk!

This now pairs up with our will to do things. We must make a conscious effort to remove the negative. This may also tie into our emotions, as some of those negative things in our lives have left scars that still need some healing. Again, our minds are very complex, and our will and emotions play into that. We all have had some kind of baggage in our lives that we have carried around for one reason or another. It is not going to get any better, though, until we make that conscious effort of our will to make it better. You are the only one who can decide to get up off the couch and do something positive with your life. Can you see how all of it ties into each other?

Our conscious mind pairs up with our will, also maybe overwriting our unconscious mind and our emotions to make ourselves better. It's no wonder that Psychologists get paid so much. However, as I just stated, you must choose to do all of it! I am not saying that you should not seek help for certain things. As stated, they can be very complicated, but until you have had enough of your circumstances and make that decision to change, it doesn't matter who you are talking about getting help from; you must be the one to take the action. Now, I also believe that through God all things are possible, and He can help you with whatever you are going through. You, however, need to still make that choice to seek Him for help.

I hope that briefly covering this helps and you have gained some understanding of the complexity of our minds. The last part of the mind that I want to cover here is much the same. Our minds can be told things to us by God and the Holy Spirit. We need to understand how to hear from God. This links us to our own spirit. Also, sometimes with that knowledge, we then need to have our minds tell our bodies what to do. All of this you can see is linked and complex.

Spirit:

God breathed life into us which is our spirit. This is spoken about first thing in the bible in Genesis 2:7, *And the LORD God formed man of the dust of the ground, and breathed into his nostrils the breath of life; and man became a living being.*

This breath of life is the spirit we have. God spoke everything else into existence, but with us He got His hands dirty and breathed into us to make us whole. We are made in His image and likeness. First and foremost, we are spirit. We need to understand that we are not our bodies. We are a spiritual being that has a body that we call home.

This is shown to us in 2 Corinthians 5:6-8, *[6] So we are always confident, knowing that while we are at home in the body we are absent from the Lord. [7] For we walk by faith, not by sight. [8] We are confident, yes, well pleased rather to be absent from the body and to be present with the Lord.*

Our bodies are only temporary. At some point in time, we are all going to die, despite some of us (including me) thinking we are going to live forever. But those of us who choose to follow Christ get to live forever in heaven, though we don't keep this current body. This is because we are spiritual beings. Once we leave this mortal plane we then, as the scripture says, are then with God in Heaven.

There is a lot that we can talk about when it comes to us being spiritual beings. Many times, in the gospels, Jesus is recorded casting out demons from people. This is one of the main things that we need to understand when it comes to being a spirit living in a body. Just like us choosing to follow Christ, some people choose or are led astray and end up following the devil and some do not know what they are doing. We need to be careful what we allow ourselves to open up to. There is a spiritual realm that most of us do not see, know, or understand much about. This is an important reason why it is so important for us to have a close relationship with God.

A good example of this can be found in Daniel 10:12-14, *12 Then he said to me, "Do not fear, Daniel, for from the first day that you set your heart to understand, and to humble yourself before your God, your words were heard; and I have come because of your words. 13 But the prince of the kingdom of Persia withstood me twenty-one days; and behold, Michael, one of the chief princes, came to help me, for I had been left alone there with the kings of Persia. 14 Now I have come to make you understand what will happen to your people in the latter days, for the vision refers to many days yet to come."*

Now this gets deep into that spiritual realm and there is a lot going on here. What you need to understand here is that it is an angel talking to Daniel. The angel is telling him about the warfare that the angel encountered in the spiritual realm before getting to Daniel to deliver the answer to prayer. This passage again has a lot in it, but the main thing to get here is that God hears our prayers and sends the answer back with His angels in the spiritual realm. We can grow our spiritual relationship with God as it talked about, by humbling ourselves and setting our heart to understanding. With that in mind, we then can start to understand that answers to our prayers may take some time to get answered as there is warfare going on in the spiritual realm.

Feeding our whole self:

With all of what we just learned in mind, what then are we going to do for our bodies, minds, and our spirits? For us to have true balance in our lives we need to be looking at each of these areas and make sure that we are feeding and taking care of the needs of each part of who we are. I want to give you some ideas to go on as a baseline.

To help give you the balance you need in life, it is important to focus on yourself some, which will allow you to also help others in the long term. You will need to figure out what time works best for you in this, but I would suggest that you do it first thing in the morning, as there are even studies out there that show this is the best time and will give you the best overall results, and yes that is to all areas of who you are, body, mind and spirit.

Give yourself one hour every day to focus on this and you will be glad you did. Now this may sound like a lot, and you may be thinking about losing sleep or something, but if you do what I am suggesting, chances are good that you will actually sleep better, be more relaxed and have a better overall attitude about life. Let me explain further.

Though I said an hour, what I want you to do is focus just 20 minutes on each area. This is easy if you are already used to working out, as many people do for more than 20 minutes. Also, as you are working out for those 20 minutes, you can also be doing one of the other areas.

Take 20 minutes to learn something that will keep your mind active. Many of us watch videos for entertainment, so why not take that time and aim at something that will give you some knowledge in an area that you like or want to learn about? Doing this simple activity will not only give you the knowledge to work off but may even give you some motivation that you need.

Lastly but probably most importantly and often overlooked, we need to feed our spirits. Just 20 minutes a day focusing on God will build up your spirit. Now maybe 20 minutes isn't enough to get in worship, read your bible and pray, but you must start somewhere. You can always take this and build upon it. It is just important to get into a habit of doing this first before scaling up.

With any of this, it is just to give you a baseline to work from as each person is different and needs to figure out some of the details to make things work in your life. You may have to move some things around and make different priorities but trust me, a little restructuring can sometimes be just what you need to get on the right track and make the change that will allow you to accomplish your goals. For example, many of us commute to work or something most days for more than 20 minutes. You can use that time to build yourself up in your spirit or your mind.

<u>Question time</u>:

What are you going to do for your Body every day?

What are you going to do for your Mind every day?

What are you going to do for your Spirit every day?

CHAPTER 4

What are We Going to Become

The choice is always up to us as to what we are going to become in life. Now that we have started to figure out who we are and have started to develop a routine to properly build ourselves up. We need to now take things a step further and put some more action behind it.

We are now going to start talking about our Goals, Dreams, and Visions and how they apply to our lives. First, let's see what God says in Habakkuk 2 verses 1-4,

I will stand my watch

And set myself on the rampart,

And watch to see what He will say to me,

And what I will answer when I am corrected.

2 Then the LORD answered me and said:

"Write the vision

And make it plain on tablets,

That he may run who reads it.

3 For the vision is yet for an appointed time;

But at the end it will speak, and it will not lie.

Though it tarries, wait for it;

Because it will surely come,

It will not tarry.

4 "Behold the proud,

His soul is not upright in him;

But the just shall live by his faith.

There is a lot going on in this passage, but did you notice in the first verse about correction? God will tell us when we are doing something wrong or just going down the wrong path that is not the direction that He has for us. That is one of the biggest things that the Holy Spirit does for us. The Holy Spirit is there to lead us and guide us. There can be times when we need to make some corrections. God does this because He loves us, and

He only wants the best things for us. The Bible talks about God giving us the desires of our hearts, but we need to make sure that we are also staying humble and lining up with His word and not going down the wrong path that would cause the correction.

The biggest underlying principle here in this passage is Patience! When I was younger, I used to say that if God wanted me to have Patience, He would have made me a doctor. The funny thing is I now have a Doctorate, so I guess I have patience, lol. Now, maybe I was trying to be a little funny in saying that, but to some degree, it was true. At least for me, when I was younger, patience was something I struggled with. Maybe you can relate? Not that I have it all figured out currently by any means, but I feel that along the way, God has helped me and given me the tools I needed to help grow in this area.

Many of us have heard 1 Corinthians 13 at a wedding before. When I first got saved, I was given a bible that was an NIV (New International Version).

Here is 1 Corinthians 13 verse 4 in the NIV, *Love is patient, love is kind. It does not envy, it does not boast, it is not proud.*

I had a really hard time reading this when I was younger. If Love is patient, then what chance did I have? Over time, though, something interesting happened. As I would help people with different things (mostly computers) people would say to me how patient I was. I would chuckle to myself. Also, I had a hard time accepting compliments, not knowing what to say, so I would maybe softly say, "Thanks." By the way I am not a softly speaking person, as I can be in the front of a room and talk to someone in the back clearly. Ok, I am loud, lol. Most of this had to do with how I grew up. Anyway, I say all of this to hopefully give you an example of Patience and why it is so important to our lives and what we want to accomplish in them.

Back now to the passage in Habakkuk. This is now the part where we are going to start doing something. It said, "Write the vision and make it plain on tablets."

These are two different things, and we will cover them both, but I want you to start writing out your dreams, goals, and visions. Now, this may prove to be a bit challenging, but once you get going, it will start to flow. To get started with this, I want you to write down anything that comes to mind, no matter how wild or out there it is. If you do not have anything on hand to write on, there is a section in the back of the book where I put some journal pages where you can start to write down your goals.

Make sure to cover all the different aspects of your life and not just personal. Put down anything and everything. Do you have business things you want to do? Maybe God is speaking to you about some ministry you can do. By the way, we all are part of the body of Christ and each of us has a function to provide. You do not need to be a pastor or other higher function of a church to be just as effective in reaching a person and touching their lives. Just write down all your Goals, Dreams, and Visions, even if it is to tour the world on a cruise. Your list could be a hundred different things, doesn't matter how much or even how little. Stop here and start writing things down and then come back for what to do next.

Question time:

Did you write down your goals yet?

What did you learn about your goals?

How many different areas did you cover?

57

CHAPTER 5

Where are We Going to Go

Now that we have put pen to paper and started to think about our Goals and life more, where are we going to go with all of this? We can't always choose what happens to us, but we get to choose what happens afterward. There are so many different things that we could cover, but I want to try and give you some basics as I did with patience, so you have something that you can build from.

Now that you have been thinking about your goals and getting all excited about them, let's figure out how to handle them properly. Part of what I mean by this is when should we say something and maybe get someone to help us vs. not saying anything at all.

We see an example of this first in Matthew 17:5-9, *5 While he was still speaking, behold, a bright cloud overshadowed them; and suddenly a voice came out of the cloud, saying, "This is My beloved Son, in whom I am well pleased. Hear Him!" 6 And when the disciples heard it, they fell on their faces and were greatly afraid. 7 But Jesus came and touched them and said, "Arise, and do not be afraid." 8 When they had lifted up their eyes, they saw no one but Jesus only. 9 Now as they came down from the mountain, Jesus commanded them, saying, "Tell the vision to no one until the Son of Man is risen from the dead."*

Where there may be more to this passage, we need to set the stage a bit to clarify the last verse and how it may apply. Sometimes God will show you or tell you something that is just for you at the time. We can still move forward with something that God shows us, but not broadcast it to the world until it is the proper time that God gives us the green light. With all you have written down some of those things may take some planning and will require help along the way, but make sure that in all you do, you keep God first and He will direct your path. Now of course some of your goals are built on others and this is a good thing. God will bring us the help when we need it. If we are staying lined up with God, He will tell us what is right for us to do now and what things need to wait.

I want to show you the other side of things also so you can fully understand what actions you need to take and when. We see this in Acts 18:9-11, *9 Now the Lord spoke to Paul in the night by a vision, "Do not be afraid, but speak, and do not keep silent; 10 for I am with you, and no one will attack you to hurt you; for I have many people in this city." 11 And he continued there a year and six months, teaching the word of God among them.*

We see in this passage a few different things. One is not to be afraid. This alone is a major thing. With anything in life, you can only be on one side of the fence and no walking on the fence either. To that, then, I always like to say that you can only ever be in one thing, fear, or faith. Maybe you can replace faith with something else that is positive as it applies to whatever the current situation is. The point, though, is that fear is not good, and it will not allow you to reach your goals and dreams as it will keep you from getting out there and applying yourself.

In contrast to the other passage, this one shows us that God is saying to do it now! Therefore, it is important for us to seek God first and pray about all our Goals, Dreams, and Visions that we have for our lives and all the different aspects that they are a part of. Things may be scary at times, and you may get nervous about sticking your neck out there, but as we see in this passage, it says God will be with you and not to fear. Do not let fear rule over you. If you are following what God has told you to do and when, you will not have anything to fear at all.

Now that we understand that we need to seek after God's direction and do things in His timing and not fear, what's next? I want you to now take your list of goals and prioritize them if you have not already done so. To be clear, I want you to take the list and break up the various aspects, like personal, business, ministry, whatever you have and rewrite them down under those headings. Then I also want you to prioritize them starting with whatever is the biggest goal you want to achieve. Keeping in mind, though this may be your number one priority, it may take some time to see it come to pass. Make sure that as you are going over this list again, you are talking to God about all these goals. You may even get more, which is fine. Write them down also. Be prepared, though, if God does some correcting and certain ones need to be removed.

Question time:

What are the different areas that you came up with?

Did God speak to you about what you need to do now?

Did God tell you what you need to wait on?

What steps can you start to plan and see some of your goals start to fall into place?

CHAPTER 6

More to the Story

There is always more to the story. There are so many things that we can talk about when it comes to your Goals, Dreams, and Visions for your life. Before we get to the next step of what to do now that you have a prioritized list of categories. I want to give you some insight into how people will harm you and/or help you in your goals.

The following passage shows us how God uses one person to impact another.

Acts 9:10-19, [10] Now there was a certain disciple at Damascus named Ananias; and to him the Lord said in a vision, "Ananias."

And he said, "Here I am, Lord."

[11] So the Lord said to him, "Arise and go to the street called Straight, and inquire at the house of Judas for one called Saul of Tarsus, for behold, he is praying. [12] And in

a vision he has seen a man named Ananias coming in and putting his hand on him, so that he might receive his sight."

13 Then Ananias answered, "Lord, I have heard from many about this man, how much harm he has done to Your saints in Jerusalem. 14 And here he has authority from the chief priests to bind all who call on Your name."

15 But the Lord said to him, "Go, for he is a chosen vessel of Mine to bear My name before Gentiles, kings, and the children of Israel. 16 For I will show him how many things he must suffer for My name's sake."

17 And Ananias went his way and entered the house; and laying his hands on him he said, "Brother Saul, the Lord Jesus, who appeared to you on the road as you came, has sent me that you may receive your sight and be filled with the Holy Spirit."18 Immediately there fell from his eyes something like scales, and he received his sight at once; and he arose and was baptized.

19 So when he had received food, he was strengthened. Then Saul spent some days with the disciples at Damascus.

This passage is interesting and shows us many things if we are looking. What I want to point out here, is how God used Ananias to impact Saul's life. Saul, who later becomes Paul and writes about two-thirds of the New Testament, would not have been able to do that had it not been for Ananias. We will impact people's lives as we go forward and complete our goals. The opposite is also true, along the way to achieving our goals, we are going to need people to come alongside of us to help. We see in the passage that Ananias did what God said, but did you also notice the part where he questioned God and was in fear? This fear thing keeps coming up. Now, rightfully so, as Saul at the time had been murdering Christians. As stated before, if God is with you will not have anything to fear.

Just to give us a little more on fear, let's look at: Genesis 15:1, *After these things the word of the LORD came to Abram in a vision, saying, "Do not be afraid, Abram. I am your shield, your exceedingly great reward."*

This backs up that we are to not be in fear, but it also shows us that God has our backs. Once we can get past our fear and move into the faith area where we trust in God; things can start to fall into place. Fear is not going to allow you to get your Goals, Dreams, and Visions completed. If you, however, can put your faith and trust in God, He will walk beside you and become that shield. There are so many things that come after us at any given time. When you are lined up with God and following His directions, as we see with Ananias, we have nothing to fear. We saw this in the last chapter also when God spoke to Paul and told him not to fear and that God would be with him.

Getting back to the people impacts part of all of this. There are things we need to be mindful of when it comes to our Goals, Dreams, and Visions for our lives. There are people that God is going to send to us, but there are people around us also that we already know that can help. Of those people, not everyone is going to go on the journey with us. This can be the hard part also. Not everyone is going to be like-minded as we talked about earlier in the book. Your heart may want to help everyone, but at the same time, you need to make sure that other people are not going to bring you down. There are times in our lives when we try to help people, but some of them may take advantage of us or just think someone else needs to take care of them and their needs. Now, I am not saying that we don't need some help ourselves or that we shouldn't try to help people. However, we need to better equip people with the tools that they need to pick themselves up and move forward in a positive way with their own lives.

The people that we take with us to help us along the way need to be where we are or close to it in their own lives. This is the only way that they will be able to see the vision we have and run with it, as it says in Habakkuk. We need to surround ourselves with like-minded people who not only have visions of their own but are positive and motivated in life. Then we are both able to help one another meet all our goals.

This is also a different mindset for us to have. We all need other people from time to time. We are not capable of doing everything ourselves. This also can help us to prioritize our time and efforts. We all have things that we are good and are bad at. You are going to need someone to help you with something along the way. Maybe not at first with the simple stuff, but as God starts to direct you and moves you into other areas that are higher; you will need others that share the vision and are positive about that will not bring you down.

This all has to do with the gifts and talents that God has given us. I often use the example in Matthew 25:14-29 (please read on your own), the Parable of the Talents. Though it talks about Talents being money, the principle here is the same. God gives us all the ability and talent to do something. Some people may be very athletic, while others are book smart, and others are skilled with their hands.

The point here again is that God had put into us these abilities as gifts. These gifts can and will develop over time and will even grow as the parable talks about the one with five got five more and the one with two got two more. Over time if we develop and nurture our gifts and talents, not only will they grow stronger, but other abilities that we did not have will start to grow. God has a way of equipping us with what we need if we are following Him and letting Him. Unfortunately, some people choose to sit around and do nothing and waste, possibly even lose their gifts as the one in the parable did with the one talent.

As you can see, this parable offers some good insight to us. If we can focus our own gifts and talents on what we are good at, along the way, we get more as we grow in our knowledge. How do we get that knowledge, though? First, start by getting those like-minded people or the others God will send your way to help. Don't think that you must do everything yourself! Utilize other people where you need to so you can focus on what God wants you to do. Not to mention what God has equipped you with. If God gave you the two talents, don't try to work on things like you got five. You will stretch yourself too thin and you will get your Body, Soul, and Spirit out of that balance we have talked about.

With all of this, and before we get to our next step, I feel that I need to give some extra insight here that may help to put our gifts and talents into more perspective. There is a lot in the bible that is taught on Knowledge, Understanding, and Wisdom. These things intertwine with our own gifts and talents to some degree, but I am sure that you can agree, we need them in every aspect of our lives.

To give them a quick basic explanation. Knowledge is something that we learn, be it through a book or taught by doing. Understanding is taking that knowledge and applying it over and over, maybe learning more about it along the way and becoming better about that thing. Wisdom is then being able to apply that understanding and show or tell others to give them knowledge. Again, there is so much more to all of this in the Bible, but the key thing that is said over and over is if you ask God for knowledge, understanding, and wisdom;

He will give it to you! Solomon did this and was mightily blessed!

Now that you have written down your goals, dreams, and visions. Prioritize them and pray to God asking for His direction. It is time to do what the other part of Habakkuk said. It is time now to "make it plain on tablets."

Get a poster board and find some pictures that go along with your goals. If you have to make the pictures or edit them to put a picture of you into the scene, then do that also. You can decide to have more than one vision board as you have multiple topics, but at least make one that has the top 10 things. Put this Vision Board somewhere you are going to see it all the time. This is what that verse means when it talks about making it plain. You want it to be so big and bold that you have to see it, so even if you are running past it quickly, you can still take in the full meaning and know what needs to be done. You do not need to write down all of the details here. That is also part of keeping it plain. God will help you fill in the blanks over time. It is okay if you have a Goal that you have no idea how you are going to accomplish. If God has brought you to it, He will get you through it. Worry is just another word for fear. We are not going to be in fear any longer!

<u>Question time:</u>

Is there any fear still holding you back?

If so, what are you going to do about it?

Is there someone that needs to cut loose so they do not bring you down?

Who do you need to take with you?

What talents do you have?

What talents do you need, and where/who will provide them?

Did you put your Vision Board in plain sight so you can see it and run?

CHAPTER 7

Be the New You

If you have followed along and completed all the steps, you have accomplished more than most people do in goal setting in their whole lives. If you can keep this up and develop this into a habit, you will Be the New You!

There is so much more that you will do and become. I want to now encourage and challenge you a bit to start keeping a journal. The challenge part here is to start doing it for the first 30 days, hopefully after which, it will become a habit. There are many ways to do journaling, of course, but I want you to focus on the goals, dreams, and visions that we have been talking about. Every day write down what is on your heart and what you have been talking about with God. This is going to change from day to day, so no looking back at what you wrote the day before. Certain things have a way of changing over time. Not that you lose sight of things, but other things may become more important, or God will help you to shift your focus. After the first 30 days of journaling about your goals, then look back and see what has happened. What things changed? How far have you come?

Now, of course, things take time, so do not lose heart. Just know that in the end, God is shaping and molding you into that perfect cornerstone that He can build upon. You will then be able to help guide others with what you have learned from your personal experiences.

I just mentioned personal experiences and shared them to help others. This is a simple mentoring plan. We all need to have a mentor and then hopefully later be a mentor to someone else who needs it. Finding the right mentor can take a while, but keep in mind that not everyone is going to fit all of the different areas in your life.

Just as we have different categories for our goals, likewise, those areas of our lives will require different mentors and maybe even more than one. This may seem like it will be a lot of work, but it doesn't have to be that way. Not all your mentors will you necessarily know personally. As a pastor, I look to other pastors that I may never have even met but are well known. This is not the only area in which I do this, but as I need to make sure that I am also feeding my spirit, I also look to others that I trust and know are not teaching a false doctrine. You need to find the people in the area that you need to be mentored in and listen to what they say, and how they say it, and then if everything lines up and is good, then do what they say. Do not be led astray by anyone in anything. Ensure that you are keeping things lined up with God first and foremost.

When finding a mentor, I want you to remember that even if you already know a lot, there is always more to learn. Part of having a good mentor is that they will challenge you, hopefully like this book has and get you to step out of your comfort zone. Now, if you do find a person that you can work with one-on-one, don't be surprised if you will have to pay something for their time and knowledge. This may not always be the case if you know the person well. If this happens to you, make sure that you honor them well and humble yourself as you are learning from them as a teacher who knows what they are talking about. Try to keep any personal relationship outside of this mentoring as you may need to be corrected from time to time on things and need to submit to them.

Mentoring is basically what Jesus did with the disciples. They were called disciples because they followed the teacher, who was Jesus and followed the teachings of Jesus. None of them were perfect except for Jesus, of course. He is the only one who has ever been perfect. We need to try to be like Him but do not get down on yourself if you fall and need help to get back up. The key is that you get back up!

We need to have good mentors who will take the time to show us and equip us with what we need. Even if they are ones we watch online or read their books, there is so much information out there. You may need to sift through some of it to get to the gold.

This could be part of the reason that Jesus was asked by a disciple of John this question in Matthew 9:14, *Then the disciples of John came to Him, saying, "Why do we and the Pharisees fast often, but Your disciples do not fast?"*

This shows us, in part, that not everyone teaches the same, but it's not that Jesus was teaching them wrong. There is just more of a time and place for everything.

His reply in Matthew 9:15-17 says, *15 And Jesus said to them, "Can the friends of the bridegroom mourn as long as the bridegroom is with them? But the days will come when the bridegroom will be taken away from them, and then they will fast. 16 No one puts a piece of unshrunk cloth on an old garment; for the patch pulls away from the garment, and the tear is made worse. 17 Nor do they put new wine into old wineskins, or else the wineskins break, the wine is spilled, and the wineskins are ruined. But they put new wine into new wineskins, and both are preserved."*

There is a lot to this, but like I said there, is a time and place for everything. Jesus is saying that

He is teaching them what they need as they need it to equip them for when He is gone. He does teach them later about fasting and how to do it properly. Too often, we want to have and know everything there is right away. Then, thinking we know something, we move too quickly and mess up everything.

Having a good mentor who will give you good teaching and steps to follow to equip you for success is what you need to look for. Then, also know when you need to ask a question or ask for help! A question is not stupid; only the person who does not ask it. Oh, that seems harsh, but if you haven't noticed, I have taught you how to walk already, and now you are learning more about how to run. You are going to stumble along the way, but never be in fear to ask for help or what may seem like a stupid question. You don't know what you don't know until you ask! I ask questions all the time, just as I have been asking questions of you throughout this book.

The last thing I want to challenge you about is finding a mentor. Do not just pick the easy mentors. Like if you are a man finding another man that will mentor you. All of this is fine when you are starting out, so do it some to get started, but do not stay only with them. With the example of the man, find a woman also that can mentor you. There are a lot of people online with all kinds of content. Likewise, if you are a woman, though I understand having a woman, especially one that you can talk to personally, don't give up on us Men. The reason I say this is not only to challenge us but to see things from a different perspective. We all have something to learn or offer the other.

As we are talking about that different perspective. You should then also have someone outside of your own ethnicity as they have experienced things you have not, and you can gain some valuable insight. Throughout my life, I have done this, though I did not realize it necessarily. Many people influence us throughout our lives. We now have a better opportunity to pick for ourselves the right ones for a change and decide to make something out of ourselves in Becoming the New You.

Well, I want to leave you with a final passage Philippians 3:12-16, *12 Not that I have already attained, or am already perfected; but I press on, that I may lay hold of that for which Christ Jesus has also laid hold of me. 13 Brethren, I do not count myself to have apprehended; but one thing I do, forgetting those things which are behind and reaching forward to those things which are ahead, 14 I press toward the goal for the prize of the upward call of God in Christ Jesus. 15 Therefore let us, as many as are mature, have this mind; and if in anything you think otherwise, God will reveal even this to you. 16 Nevertheless, to the degree that we have already attained, let us walk by the same rule, let us be of the same mind.*

This passage backs up a lot of what has been written here that I have said. I hope that this book has been an inspiration for you and a tool for you to continue to look back to for encouragement. As the passage says, "Press toward the goal". If you take what has been said here to heart and apply it to yourself, you will succeed.

<u>Question time:</u>

What areas do you need a mentor?

Where are you going to find that person?

Do you have that person that is going to challenge you?

Do you have multiple mentors that will give you a different perspective?

SALVATION PRAYER

Father God, I hear that you sent Jesus into this world to die for my sins. That you raised Him from the dead, and He is seated at your right hand in Heaven. Jesus, I ask that you forgive me of my sins. Come into my heart, be my Lord and Savior now and forever. Jesus, I also ask you that you would send to me the Holy Spirit to fill me and guide me all the days of my life in your Spirit of Truth. In Jesus Name, AMEN!

NOTES

Use these empty pages to write your Goals or what God is speaking to you about.

NOTES

NOTES

NOTES

NOTES

NOTES

93

ABOUT DR. DONATO PERRICCI

D r. Donato coaches and mentors people all around the world to become all that they can be. As in this book, you must start at the ground floor to move up and get higher. This goes for all walks of life and anything that you want to do. Donato specializes in the business aspect of his coaching to get people to think outside of the box and get people to think about how things will also impact the future, not just the here and now.

Dr. Donato is a Pastor, Coach, Speaker, International Best-Selling Author, Businessman, and so much more. He has been involved in many areas of ministry over the past 30 years and currently serves as the Senior Pastor in the Twin Cities Metro area of Minnesota. Dr. Donato's desire is to impact people's lives with the Gospel and with everything he teaches. Dr. Donato's goal is to inspire, encourage, and build a person up to accomplish all their goals, dreams, and visions so they can be all God created for them to become.

Dr. Donato has been a leader in Corporate America for over 30 years. He has served in many different roles, most of which involve Technology. Donato has worked for many of the top Fortune 500 companies, overseeing many multi-million-dollar projects and the people involved. All these projects have many challenges, so Dr. Donato knows the stress of life that we all go through.

Dr. Donato grew up all around the Midwest, but he and his wife, Nichol, call Minnesota their home. They are parents and grandparents and love every minute of it. They own and operate a few businesses where they provide help to people who need websites, social media support, and much more.

To learn more about how Dr. Donato can help you:

Website: www.donatomotivates.com

Email: Donato@donatomotivates.com

Dr. Donato Perricci

Leader, Motivator, Strategist

www.ingramcontent.com/pod-product-compliance
Lightning Source LLC
Chambersburg PA
CBHW040154160726
48006CB00014B/1742